Believe That You Can!

Believing in Yourself

Tana Hensley

SOCIAL AND EMOTIONAL LEARNING FOR THE REAL WORLD™

Rosen Classroom™

Can you do anything?
Yes, you can!

Believe in yourself.
You can do great things.

Believe that you can run the race.
Keep going!

Believe that you can swim.
Keep swimming!

Believe that you can win the game. Keep playing!

Believe that you can make the basket. Keep trying!

Believe that you can sing.
Keep singing!

Believe that you are smart.
Keep reading!

It might not be easy.
You might want to give up.

Just believe in yourself.
You will go far!

Words to Know

basket

game